MW00414025

THIS NOTEBOOK BELONGS TO:
Honey

I SEE 0 EGGS IN THE NEST

0 0 0 0 0 0

Zero Zero

0 0 0 0 0 0

Zero Zero

0 0 0 0 0 0

Zero Zero

0
Zero

0
Zero

I SEE 1 BEAR

1
One

1
One

I SEE 2 FOXES

2 2 2 2 2

Two Two Two

2 2 2 2 2

Two Two Two

2 2 2 2 2

Two Two Two

2
Two

2
Two

I SEE 3 COWS

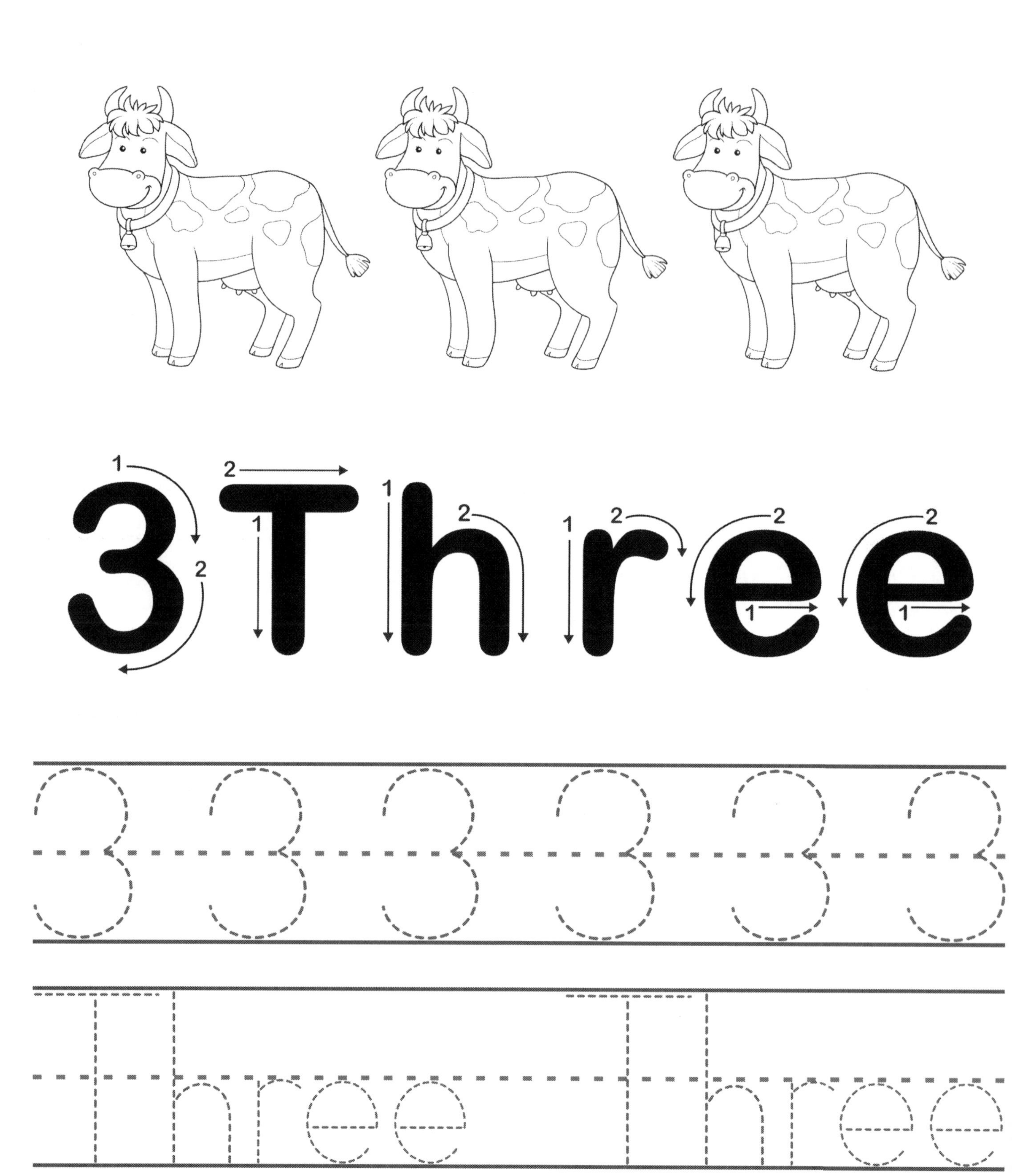

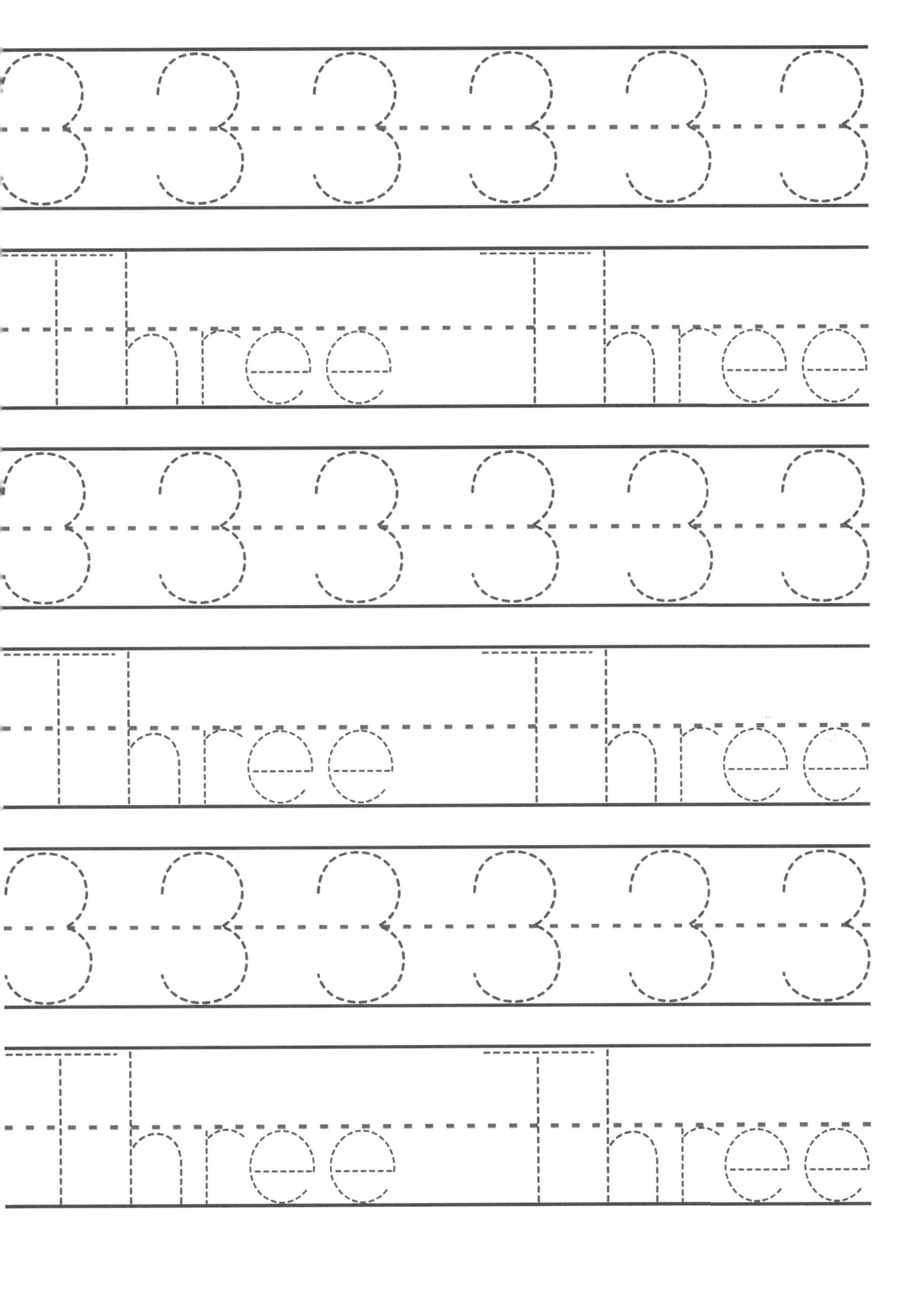
3 3 3 3 3 3
Three Three
3 3 3 3 3 3
Three Three
3 3 3 3 3 3
Three Three

3
Three

3
Three

I SEE 4 STORKS

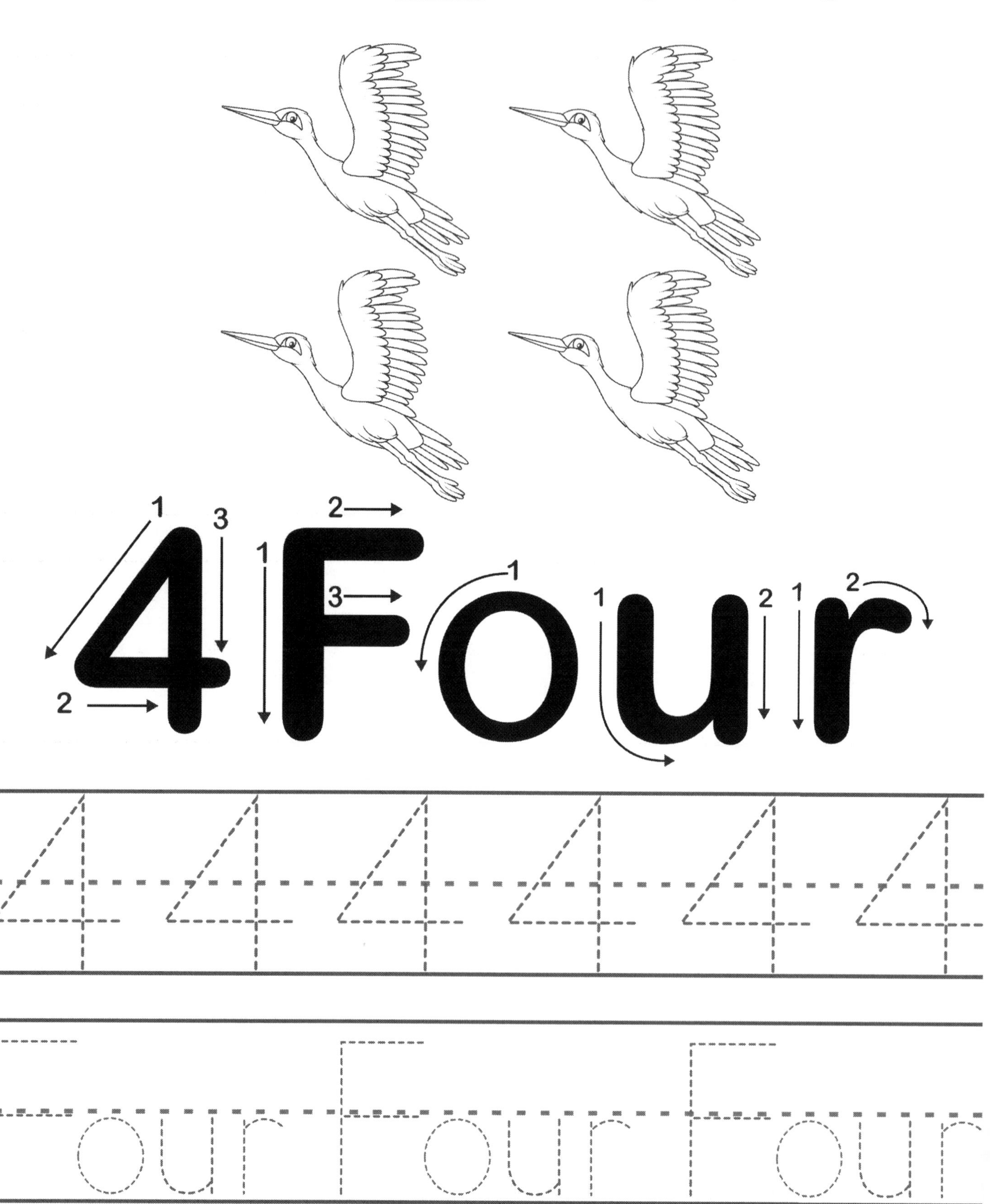

4 4 4 4 4 4

Four Four Four

4 4 4 4 4 4

Four Four Four

4 4 4 4 4 4

Four Four Four

4
Four

4

I SEE 5 PIGS

5 5 5 5 5 5

Five Five Five

5 5 5 5 5 5

Five Five Five

5 5 5 5 5 5

Five Five Five

5
Five

5
ive

I SEE 6 CAMELS

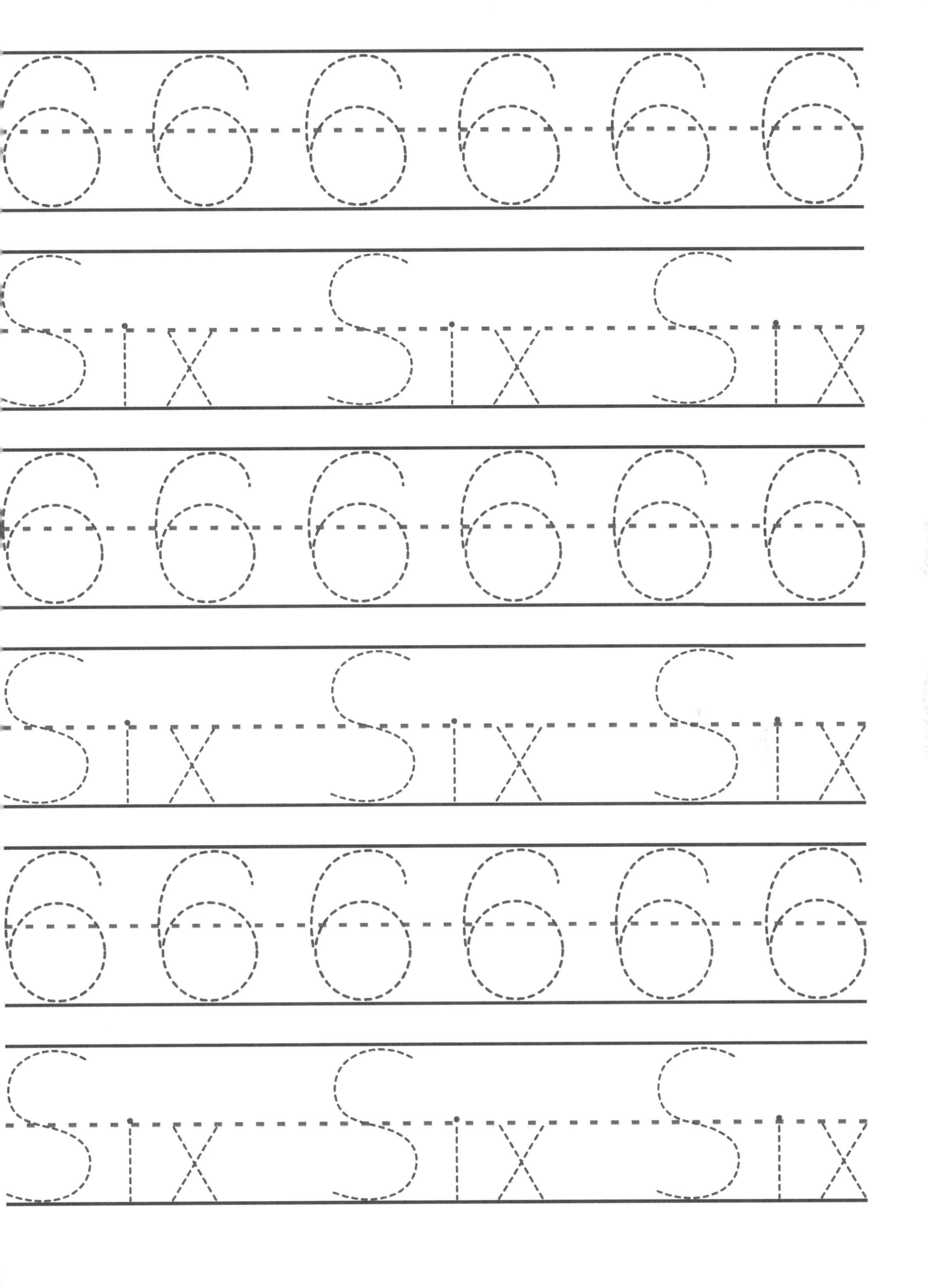
6 6 6 6 6 6
Six Six Six
6 6 6 6 6 6
Six Six Six
6 6 6 6 6 6
Six Six Six

6
Six

6
six

I SEE 7 SHEEP

7 7 7 7 7 7

Seven Seven

7 7 7 7 7 7

Seven Seven

7 7 7 7 7 7

Seven Seven

7
Seven

7
Seven

I SEE 8 MICE

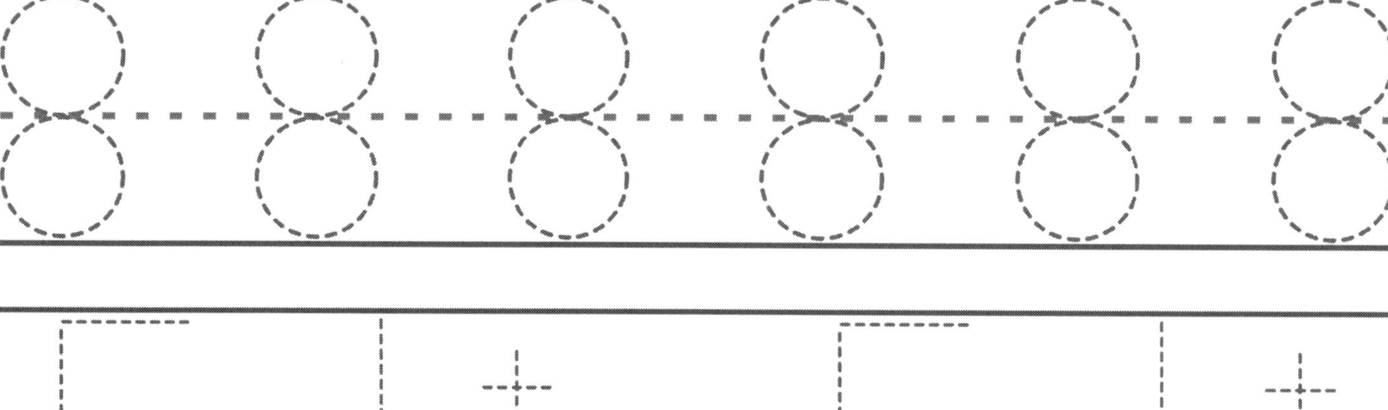

8 8 8 8 8 8

Eight Eight

8 8 8 8 8 8

Eight Eight

8 8 8 8 8 8

Eight Eight

8
Eight

8
ight

I SEE 9 BEAVERS

9 9 9 9 9 9

Nine Nine

9 9 9 9 9 9

Nine Nine

9 9 9 9 9 9

Nine Nine

9
Nine

9
Nine

I SEE 10 GEESE

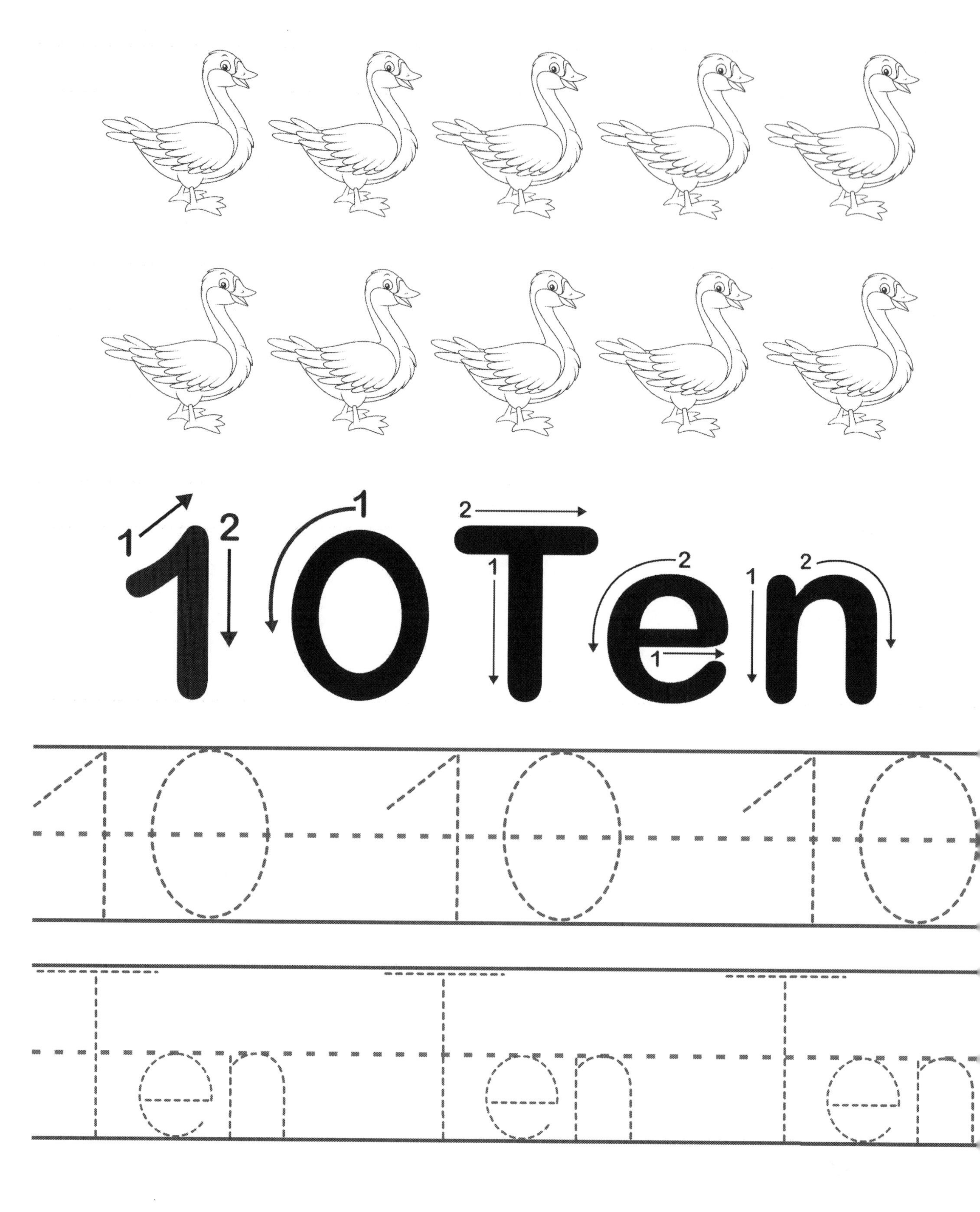

10 10 10

ten ten ten

10 10 10

ten ten ten

10 10 10

ten ten ten

I SEE 11 FROGS

11 11 11 11

Eleven Eleven

11 11 11 11

Eleven Eleven

11 11 11 11

Eleven Eleven

I SEE 12 SEALS

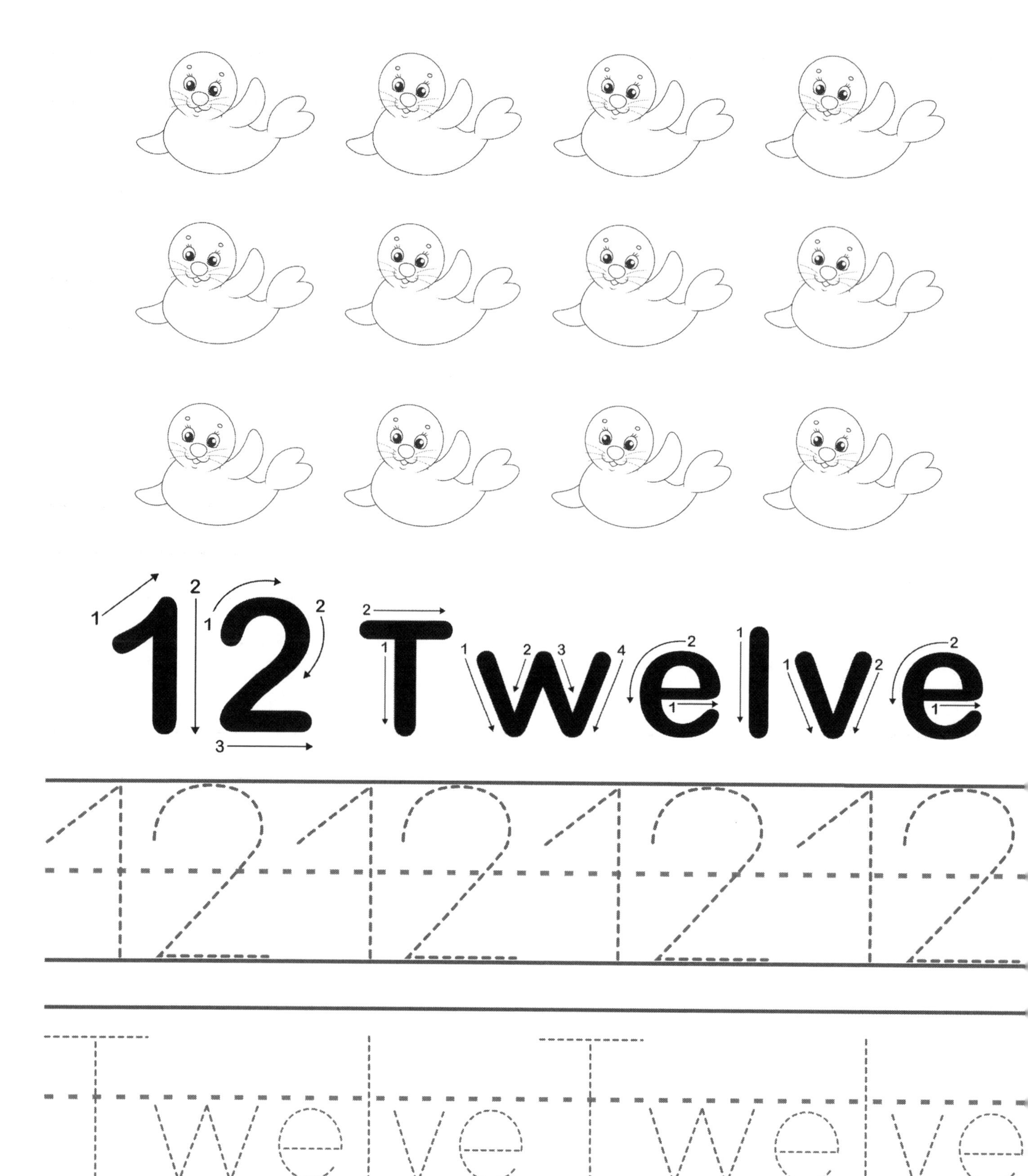

1212121212

TwelveTwelve

1212121212

TwelveTwelve

1212121212

TwelveTwelve

I SEE 13 SPARROWS

13 13 13 13

Thirteen Thirteen

13 13 13 13

Thirteen Thirteen

13 13 13 13

Thirteen Thirteen

I SEE 14 TURKEYS

14 Fourteen

14 14 14 14

Fourteen Fourteen

14 14 14 14

Fourteen Fourteen

14 14 14 14

Fourteen Fourteen

14 14 14 14

Fourteen Fourteen

I SEE 15 DEER

15 Fifteen

15 15 15 15

Fifteen Fifteen

15 15 15 15

Fifteen Fifteen

15 15 15 15

Fifteen Fifteen

15 15 15 15

Fifteen Fifteen

I SEE 16 IGUANAS

Sixteen Sixteen

16 16 16 16

Sixteen Sixteen

16 16 16 16

Sixteen Sixteen

16 16 16 16

Sixteen Sixteen

I SEE 17 EMUS

17 Seventeen

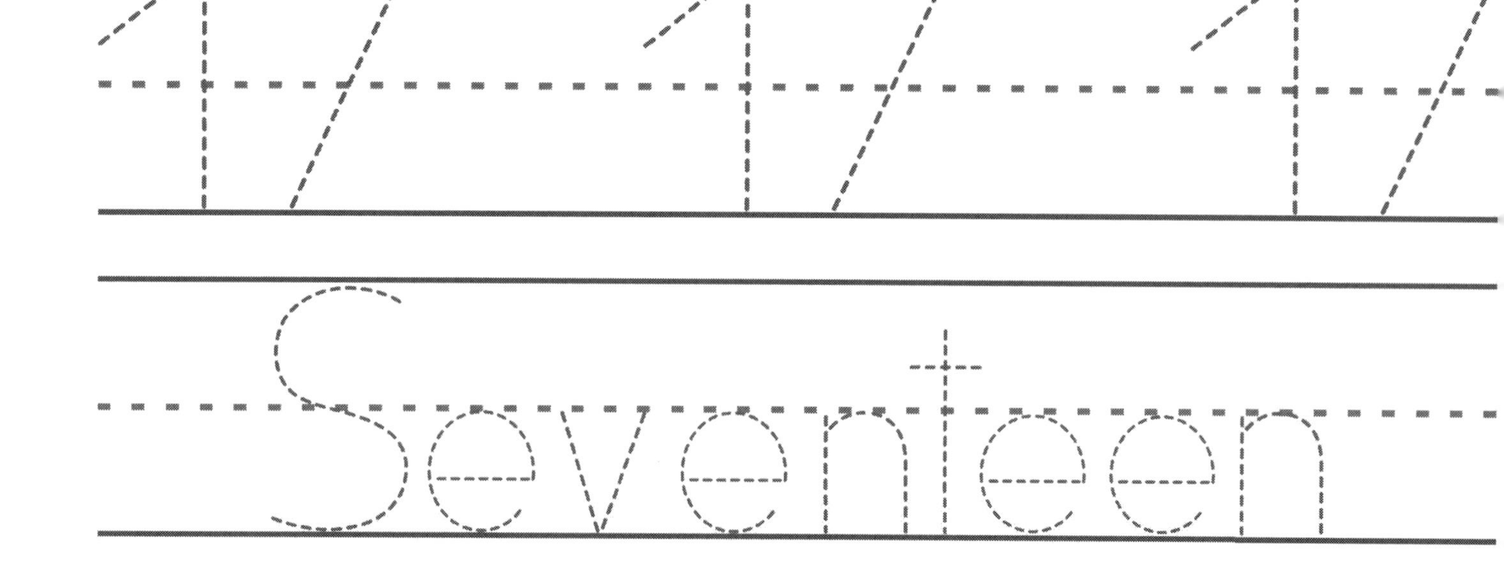

17 17 17

Seventeen

17 17 17

Seventeen

17 17 17

Seventeen

I SEE 18 RHINOS

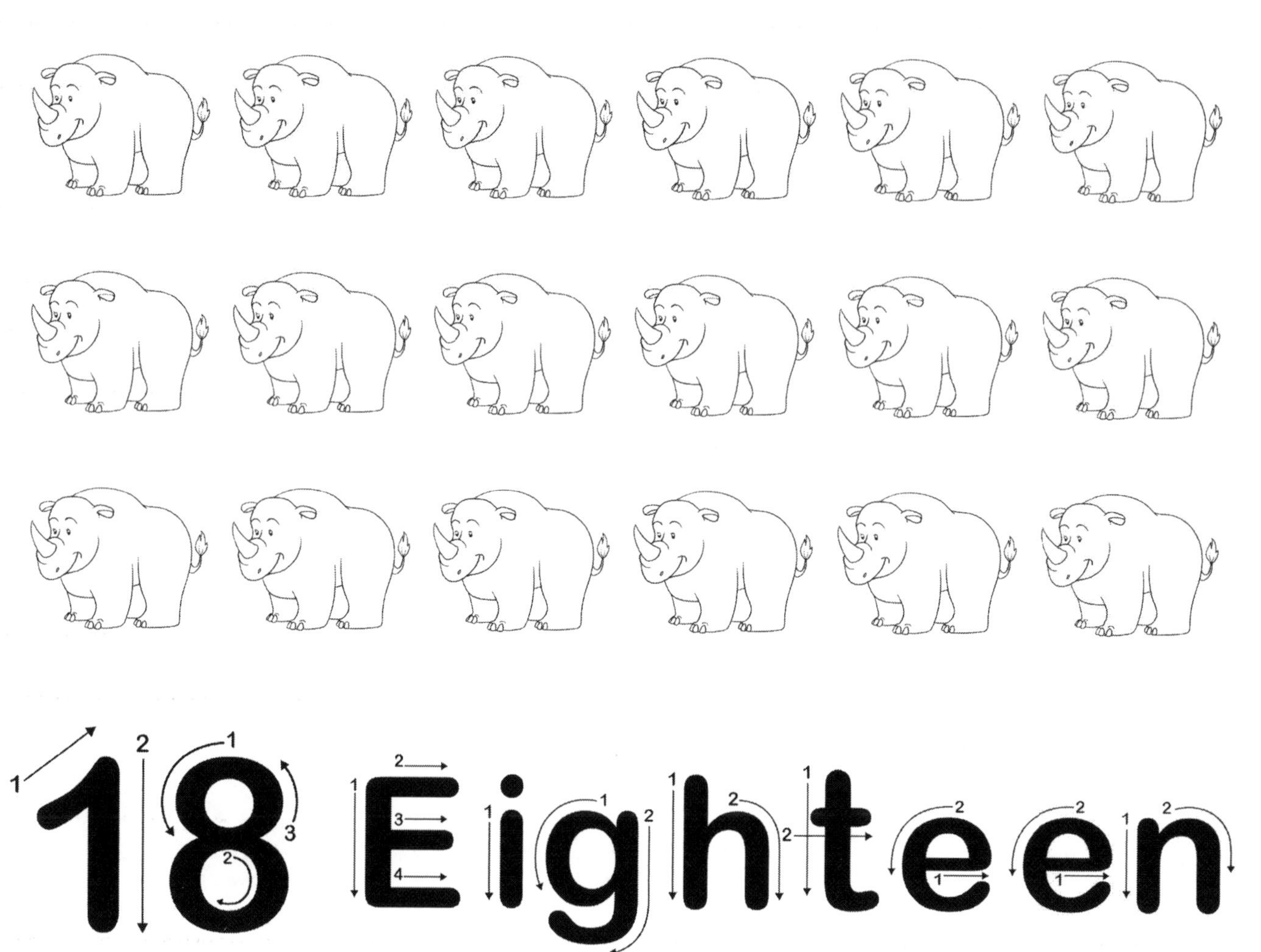

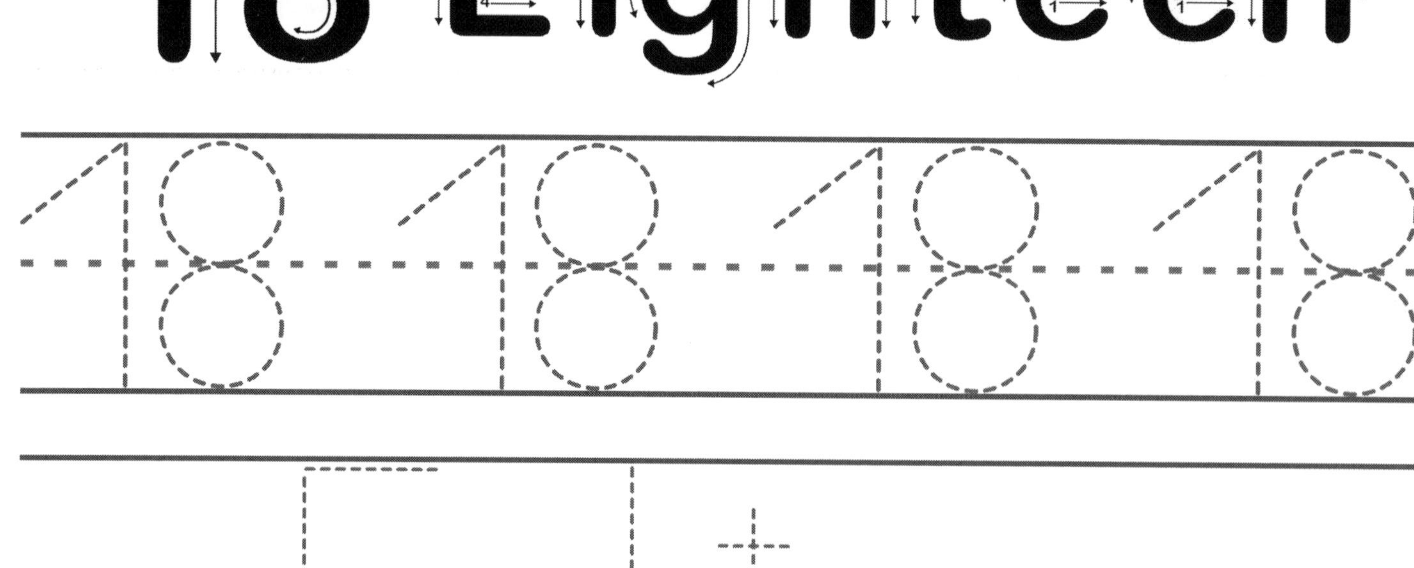

18 18 18 18

Eighteen

18 18 18 18

Eighteen

18 18 18 18

Eighteen

I SEE 19 HORSES

19 Nineteen

19 19 19

Nineteen

19 19 19

Nineteen

19 19 19

Nineteen

19 19 19

Nineteen

I SEE 20 DOGS

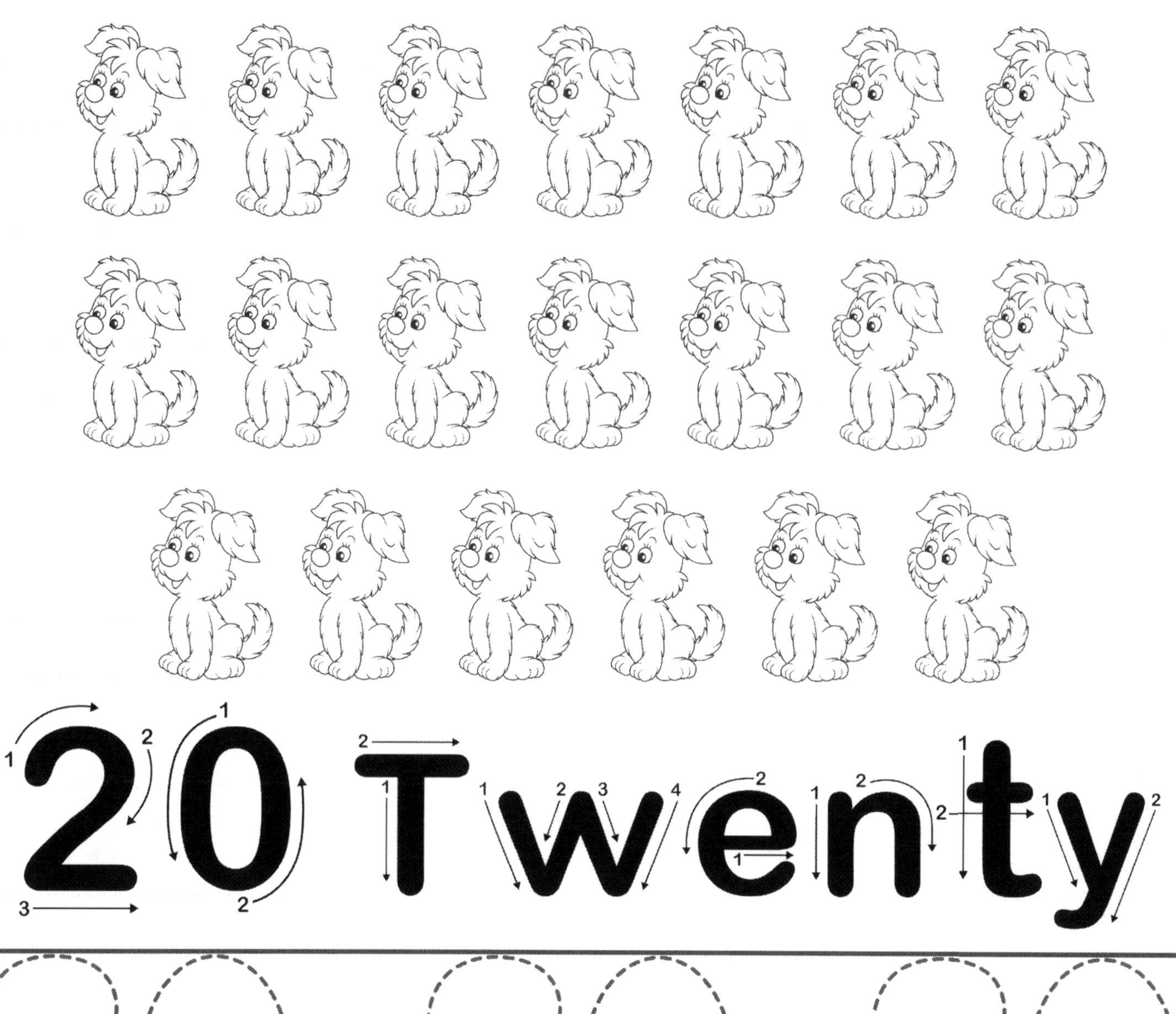

20 Twenty

20 20 20

Twenty Twenty

20 20 20

Twenty Twenty

20 20 20

Twenty Twenty

20 20 20

Twenty Twenty

LET'S RECAP THE NUMBERS

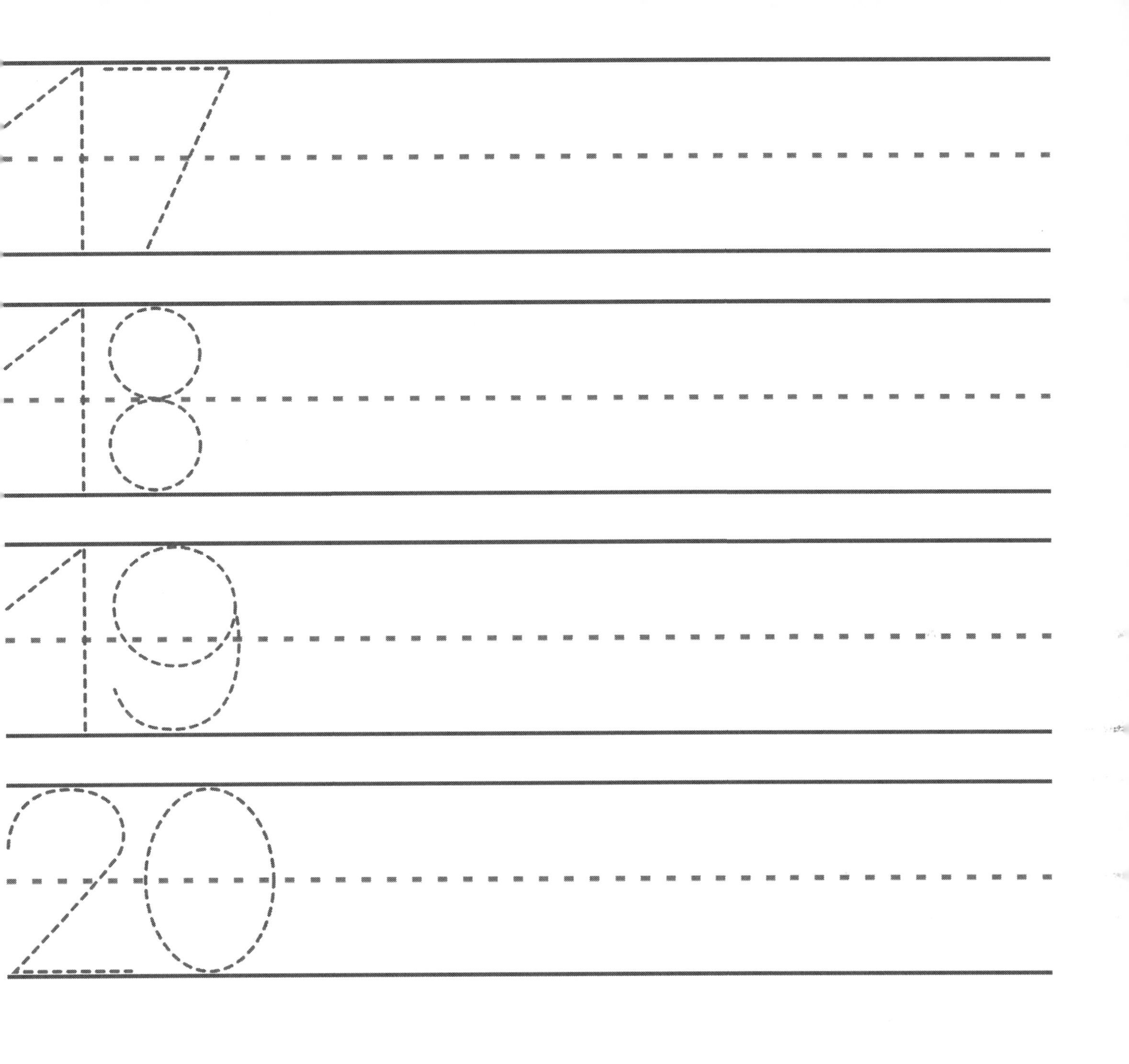

WELL DONE!

ARE YOU READY FOR THE NEXT CHALLENGE?

IT'S TIME FOR COUNTING

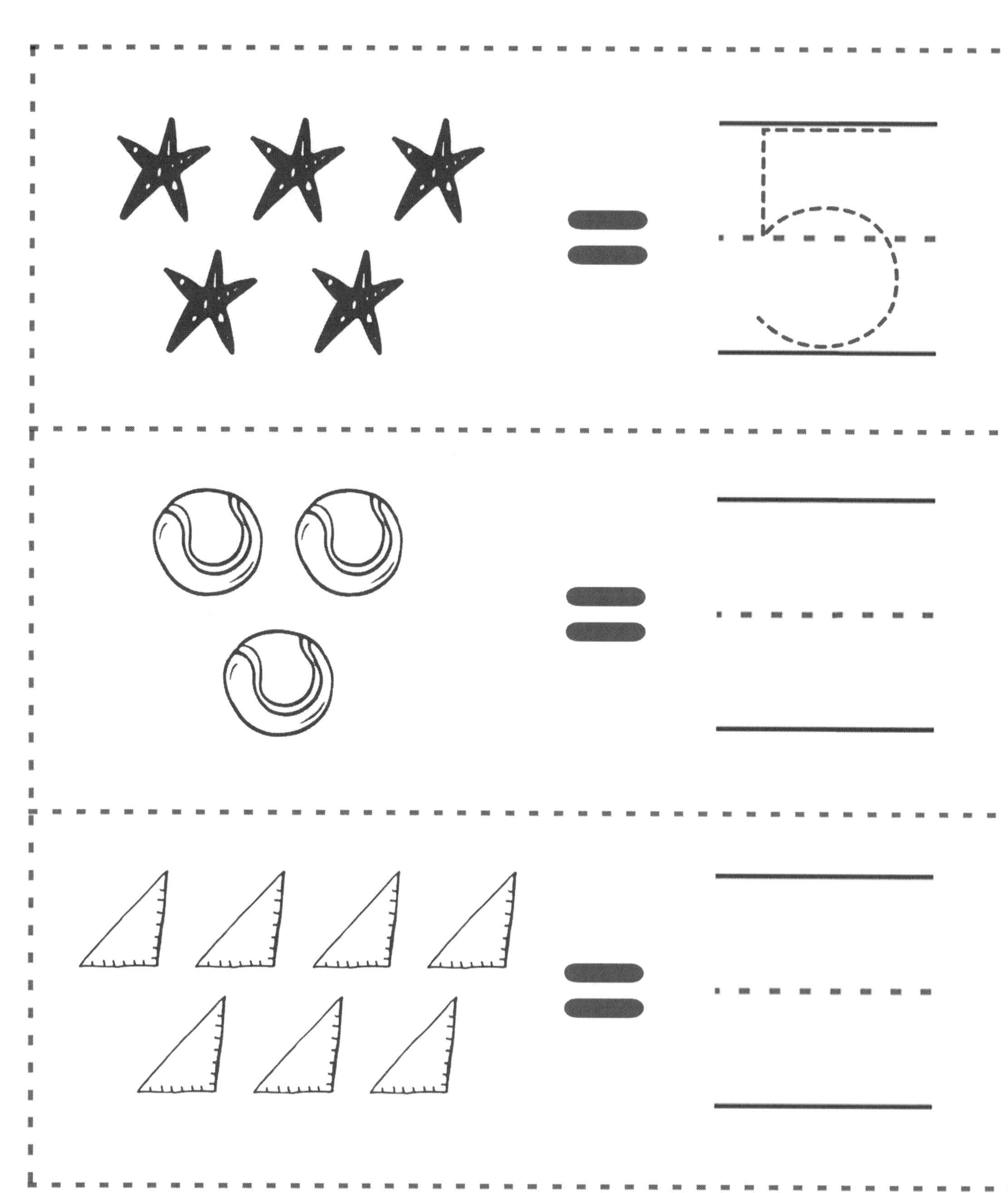

COUNT HOW MANY ITEMS YOU SEE

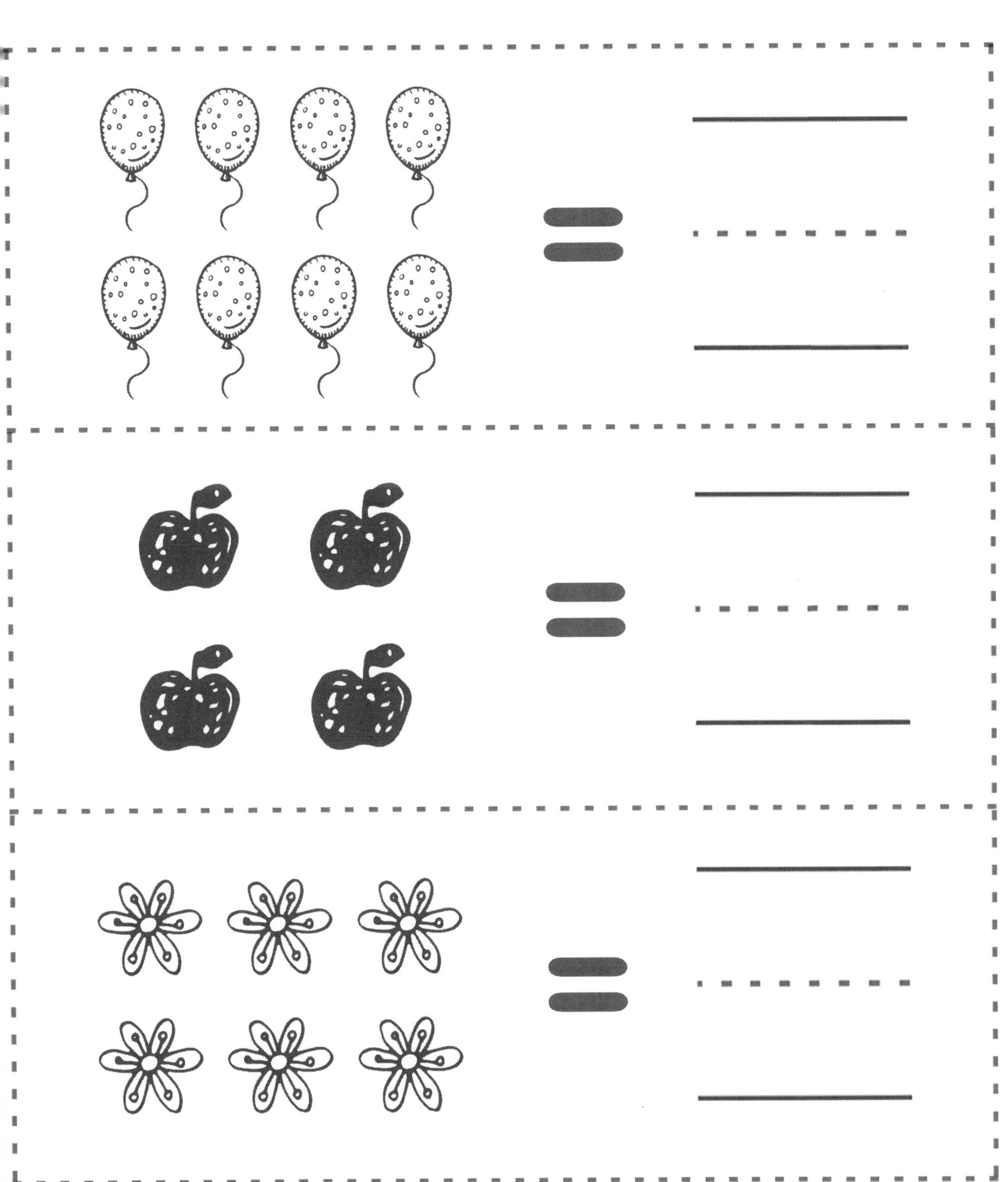

COUNT HOW MANY ITEMS YOU SEE

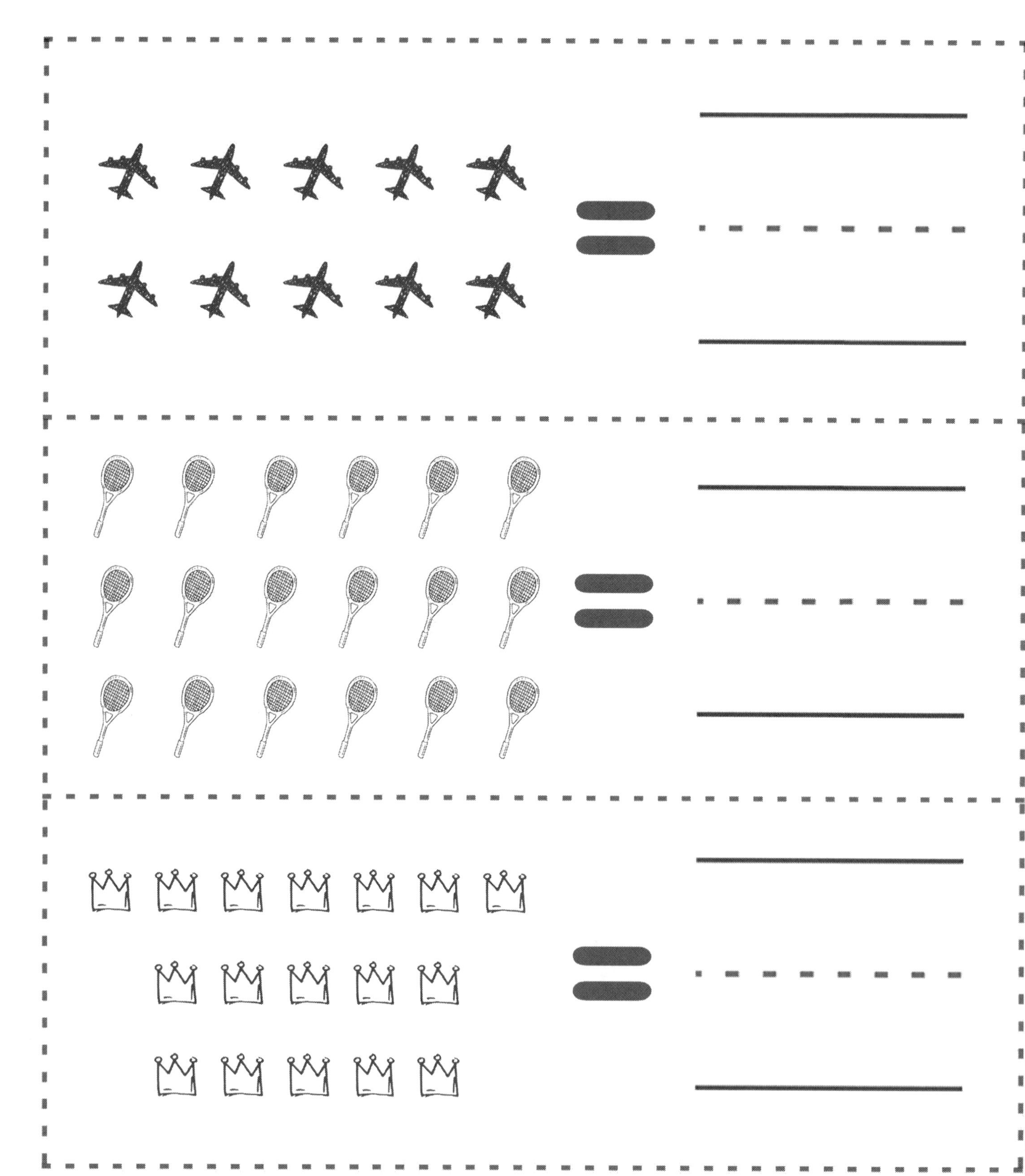

COUNT HOW MANY ITEMS YOU SEE

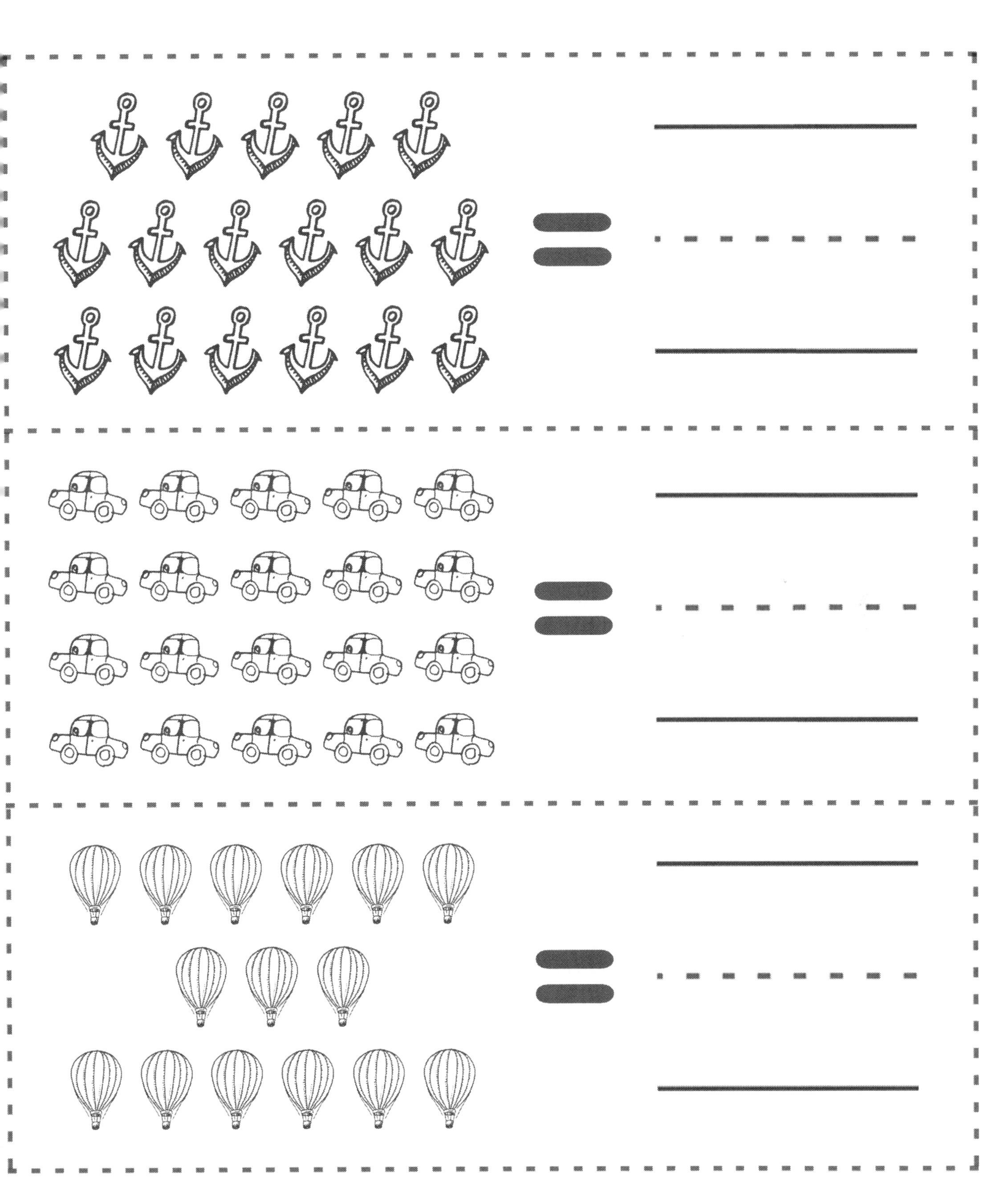

COUNT THE DOTS AND ADD THEM UP

2 + 2 = 4

3 + 4 = 7

6 + 2 = 8

COUNT THE DOTS AND ADD THEM UP

1 + 2 = ______

2 + 3 = ______

5 + 1 = ______

COUNT THE DOTS AND ADD THEM UP

$1 + 1 =$ ______

$4 + 5 =$ ______

$3 + 7 =$ ______

COUNT THE DOTS AND ADD THEM UP

$1 + 8 =$ ______

$3 + 5 =$ ______

$4 + 7 =$ ______

SIMPLE ADDITION

(YOU CAN ADD YOUR OWN DOTS BELOW THE NUMBERS TO MAKE IT EASIER)

$1+4=$ ______

$7+1=$ ______

$6+3=$ ______

SIMPLE ADDITION

(YOU CAN ADD YOUR OWN DOTS BELOW THE NUMBERS TO MAKE IT EASIER)

$2+7=$ ____

$5+6=$ ____

$2+5=$ ____

SIMPLE ADDITION

(YOU CAN ADD YOUR OWN DOTS BELOW THE NUMBERS TO MAKE IT EASIER)

$2+4=$ ______

$8+2=$ ______

$4+6=$ ______

SIMPLE ADDITION

(YOU CAN ADD YOUR OWN DOTS BELOW THE NUMBERS TO MAKE IT EASIER)

$1 + 11 =$ ______

$14 + 3 =$ ______

$17 + 2 =$ ______

SIMPLE ADDITION

(YOU CAN ADD YOUR OWN DOTS BELOW THE NUMBERS TO MAKE IT EASIER)

$5+13 =$ ______

$12+6 =$ ______

$15+4 =$ ______

SIMPLE ADDITION

(YOU CAN ADD YOUR OWN DOTS BELOW THE NUMBERS TO MAKE IT EASIER)

$2+16 =$ ______

$1+19 =$ ______

$10+4 =$ ______